ABERDEEN
CITY LIBRARIES

www.aberdeencity.gov.uk/Library
Ferryhill Library
Tel: 01224 581576
Tel: 08456 080937 or 01506 420526

Return to..

or any other Aberdeen City Library

Please return/renew this item by the last date shown
Items may also be renewed by phone or online

D1348961

ULTIMATE MILITARY MACHINES

SUBMARINES

Tim Cooke

WAYLAND
www.waylandbooks.co.uk

WAYLAND

www.waylandbooks.co.uk

First published in Great Britain in 2015 by Wayland

Copyright © 2014 Brown Bear Books Ltd.

Wayland
An imprint of Hachette Children's Group
Part of Hodder & Stoughton
Carmelite House
50 Victoria Embankment
London EC4Y 0DZ
An Hachette UK Company
www.hachette.co.uk
www.hachettechildrens.co.uk

Dewey Number: 623.8'257-dc23
ISBN: 978 0 7502 9674 8
10 9 8 7 6 5 4 3 2 1

Brown Bear Books Ltd.
First Floor
9–17 St. Albans Place
London
N1 0NX

Managing Editor: Tim Cooke
Picture Manager: Sophie Mortimer
Art Director: Jeni Child
Editorial Director: Lindsey Lowe
Children's Publisher: Anne O'Daly
Production Consultant: Alastair Gourlay

Printed in China

Picture Credits

Key: t = top, c = centre, b = bottom, l = left, r = right.

Front Cover: U.S. Navy

BAe Systemsl: 28t; John Batchelor: 06/07; National Defence, Canada: 19tl; PLAN: 27br; Robert Hunt Library: 07cr, 07br, 09tr, 13b, 16, 20, 21tl, 22cl, 23tl, 23br, 24tr, 24bl; TopFoto: Ullstein Bild 21br; U.S. Department of Defense: 05b, 10cl, 12cl, 12bc, 14tr, 15tr; U.S. Navy: 04, 06br, 08, 09b, 10br, 11cl, 11br, 13t, 14bl, 15bl, 17tl, 17bl, 18cl, 18cr, 19cr, 22br, 25tr, 25b, 26, 27tl, 29tl; Voyenno-Morskoyflot Rossii 28/29; Windmill Books: 05tl.

All Artworks: Brown Bear Books.

Brown Bear Books Ltd. has made every effort to trace copyright holders of the pictures used in this book. Anyone having claims to ownership not identified above is invited to contact: licensing@brownbearbooks.co.uk

Websites
The website addresses (URLs) included in this book were valid at the time of going to press. However, because of the nature of the internet, it is possible that some addresses may have changed, or sites may have changed or closed down since publication. While the author and publisher regret any inconvenience this may cause the readers, no responsibility for any such changes can be accepted by either the author or the publisher.

CONTENTS

INTRODUCTION

Deep beneath the world's oceans lurk some of the most powerful modern weapons: submarines. Nuclear-powered submarines patrol the seas, staying underwater for weeks at a time before they emerge to strike fear into the enemy.

USS KEY WEST

Tower, or sail, of submarine

Periscope for seeing above water when submerged

STRIKE FORCE

The U.S. Navy's underwater strike force includes Los Angeles-class nuclear-powered attack subs like the USS *Key West*. In service since 1987, this submarine carried out attacks against Afghanistan in 2001.

SPECIFICATIONS

Crew: 14 officers, 126 enlisted
Length: 110.3 m (361.9 feet)
Beam: 10 m (33 feet)
Propulsion: 1 x nuclear reactor, 1 x shaft
Max. speed: 21 knots
Displacement: 6,260 tonnes (6,900 tons)
Armament: 16 missile tubes

SUBMARINE: A vessel that can operate under the sea.

ORIGINS

Submerging powerful weapons underwater might seem like a modern idea. In fact, military submarines are over 200 years old. During the American Revolution (1775–1783), inventors came up with ways of 'sailing' beneath the water.

TURTLE

In 1776 American inventor David Bushnell used his egg-shaped wooden vessel, *Turtle* (left), to try to sink the British warship HMS *Eagle*. He failed, but the military submarine was born.

WORLD WARS

Subs played a key role in both World Wars. In World War I (1914–1918), German U-boats sank supply ships in the Atlantic. In World War II (1939–1945), U.S. submarines in the Pacific helped force the Japanese to surrender.

▲ A German U-boat patrols the North Atlantic in World War II; the U-boats targeted merchant ships.

U-BOAT: Short for 'Unterseeboot', a German submarine.

WHAT IS A SUBMARINE?

Submarines, or 'subs', are ocean-going vessels that operate fully under the water's surface. A modern submarine can remain underwater for months without surfacing. As well as carrying weapons, they have to carry all the supplies that the crew might need.

SILENT SERVICE

Hidden submarines approach silently and attack without warning. Huge vessels patrol the oceans, carrying ballistic or nuclear missiles. They can strike targets from hundreds of kilometres away.

Tower, or sail, the only part of the submarine visible above the water

USS SEAWOLF

Torpedoes stored on board

Hull made from strong steel

▲ The crew of the USS *Thresher*, one of the U.S. Navy's first nuclear attack subs, died in 1963 when the vessel sank during sea trials.

BALLISTIC: A long-range, unmanned projectile.

USS SEAWOLF

The fastest tactical submarines in the U.S. Navy are the Seawolf class. Their job is to attack enemy submarines. The USS *Seawolf* carries 130 crew on board.

SHORT OF SPACE

A large submarine is about 168 m (550 feet) long and 12.2 m (40 feet) wide. Most of the space is needed to store weapons and supplies, or for engines, so the crew fit in wherever there is space. Sometimes they sleep next to the missiles.

Bunks for the crew

Propeller

X-CRAFT AND *TIRPITZ*

Even tiny submarines can be deadly. In September 1943, during World War II, the British targeted the German battleship *Tirpitz*. Six X-Craft midget subs (top right) sailed to Norway. Each had a crew of just six men. They found and attacked the *Tirpitz* (right). The damage kept the battleship out of the war for a year.

TACTICAL: Relating to smaller, short-term operations against the enemy.

SUBMARINE MISSION

Submarines can be both tactical and strategic weapons. As tactical weapons, they can destroy specific enemy ships. In a strategic role, submarines use their long-range weapons to threaten any enemy with an attack.

COAST CLEAR

An officer on board the attack submarine USS *Norfolk* checks the ocean surface through a periscope. If there are no hostile vessels in sight, the submarine will rise to the surface.

HUNT 'N' KILL

The U.S. Navy's fast attack submarines are tactical weapons. These 'hunter-killers' carry torpedoes and missiles. Their task is to sink enemy ships.

PERISCOPE: A tube with mirrors for observing the ocean surface.

▶ By operating in small groups, submarines can increase their firepower.

"Of all branches of men in the forces, there is none which shows more devotion and faces grimmer perils than submariners."
SIR WINSTON CHURCHILL

MISSILE PLATFORM

A key job of submarines like USS *Memphis* (below) is to fire long-range missiles. Nuclear missiles are strategic weapons that threaten a whole country. Non-nuclear missiles are used to destroy military targets.

NUCLEAR: Powered by energy created by splitting or colliding atoms.

MISSILES

Submarine missiles can be fitted with nuclear warheads. They act as a deterrent. Submarines also fire non-nuclear ballistic missiles.

BALLISTIC MISSILES

A ballistic missile fired from a submarine explodes over the ocean. Non-nuclear long-range ballistic missiles from submarines can strike at almost any target, on land or sea.

▼ A Tomahawk cruise missile is launched from the USS *La Jolla*, a nuclear-powered attack submarine.

CRUISE MISSILES

Long-range cruise missiles can be nuclear or conventional. Conventional missiles are non-nuclear. They take out military targets. Nuclear missiles could wipe out whole cities. They are carried on board as a deterrent.

DETERRENT: A threat that stops someone from acting.

OTHER ROLES

Submarines are not only missile platfoms. They are used for research, transportation or patrolling the seas. They are ideal for secret missions, such as spying.

SECRET STRIKE

Submarines are a great way to deliver special forces for secret missions. Here, a U.S. Navy SEAL leaves a sub to make his way to a rigid rubber craft (RRC) on the surface.

Research submarines are used to test new military equipment. They can also gather information about the enemy. They are vital for monitoring the environmental health of the oceans and the seabed.

SEAL DELIVERY

HELPING OUT

The submersible *Mystic* is carried on the deck of a larger sub. Such deep-sea rescue vessels are used when subs get trapped, even at depths of 1,535 m (5,000 feet).

SUBMARINE FIREPOWER

Submarines carry weapons designed to attack and destroy targets at sea and on land. Torpedoes and missiles are long-distance weapons. Mines blow up closer targets.

TRIDENT

NUCLEAR REDUCTION

In the 1970s, the Strategic Arms Limitation Talks reduced the total number of nuclear weapons held around the world. Under the terms of the agreement, the U.S. Navy got rid of many of its nuclear weapons.

POSEIDON

TRIDENT

A Trident ballistic missile is launched from the USS *Nevada*. Trident can hit targets as far as 6,400 km (4,000 miles) away and has more than one warhead.

◀ The submarine USS *Will Rogers* launches a Poseidon C-3 ballistic missile. The Poseidon was used by NATO for over 40 years.

WARHEAD: The explosive part of a missile.

TORPEDOES

Torpedoes travel through the water. They can pierce a ship below the waterline, causing it to sink as the water rushes in. They are driven by an electric motor at the back and steered by a guidance system in the centre. The front section holds the explosives.

▲ Since the early 20th century, various torpedoes have been the main strike weapons carried by submarines.

▲ The crew of a surfaced U-boat watches as a merchant ship that the sub has just torpedoed sinks beneath the water.

WORLD WAR II

From 1940 to 1943, German U-boats sank 20% of Allied supply ships. They almost starved Britain into surrender. For protection, Allied ships began sailing in convoys.

CONVOY: A group of vessels or vehicles all travelling in formation.

MISSILE READY

As technology has advanced, missiles have become the most widely used submarine weapons. Vessels do not even have to surface to fire their missiles. They can be fired from deep beneath the war to hit distant targets.

● TOMAHAWK

● SHIP MISSILE

SUBHARPOON

Subharpoons are radar-guided anti-ship missiles. They can hit targets up to 128 km (80 miles) away. Guided by radar, they are hard to spot because they fly close to the surface of the sea.

◀ A Tomahawk cruise missile speeds away after being launched from a submarine. Subs can carry dozens of missiles and launch them almost simultaneously.

RADAR: A detection system that works by using radio waves.

SENSORS

When they are submerged, submarines rely on sensor systems to 'see' what is happening above or below the water. Crew on the control deck watch radar screens for signs of any enemy vessels.

▲ Sonar technicians listen on headphones on board the guided-missile destroyer the USS *The Sullivans*. Sonar uses sound waves to locate underwater objects. It is used to listen for enemy submarine activity and also for the sounds of marine mammals.

SEA MINES

Some submarines release sea mines. These floating bombs explode if enemy ships or submarines touch their prongs. It takes a lot of pressure to set them off, so divers are safe.

SUBMARINE CREW

Living on a submarine doesn't suit everyone. The crew must go without daylight or fresh air. They have to live in cramped conditions without feeling claustrophobic. They also have to get on well with their colleagues.

SILENCE PLEASE

Submariners also have to be able to be quiet. When two submarines are stalking each other, the slightest sound can give them away. Even the turn of a screw is enough for an enemy sonar operator to work out a sub's position.

LISTENING HARD

During World War II, a German U-boat crewmember listens for an enemy ship overhead. Submarine engines were noisier then, but sonar equipment was also far more basic.

CLAUSTROPHOBIC: Not liking enclosed spaces.

USS SEAWOLF

◀ The crew is on watch in the main control centre.

"Knowing the types of sounds and what to listen for takes skill."
JOHN ROONEY, PETTY OFFICER, IST CLASS

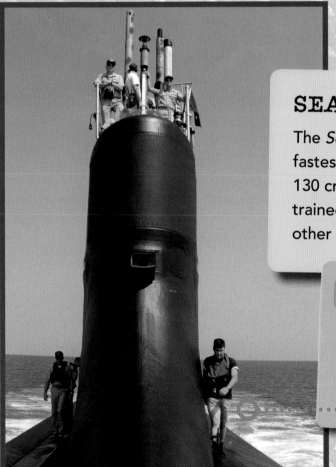

SEA STALKER

The *Seawolf* is the U.S. Navy's fastest tactical submarine. Its 130 crewmembers are specially trained to locate and attack other submarines.

SEA TRIALS

The crew takes position on the sail and deck of the USS *Seawolf* during trials in 2002.

WATCH: A naval word for a shift, or a period of time spent at work.

SUBMARINE JOBS

Everyone on a submarine has a specific role. The crew are split into departments, commanded by the Executive Department. Engineering looks after the engines; Combat Systems is in charge of weapons; Navigation and Operations steers the ship and handles communications. Submarine training is more demanding than for most other armed forces.

▲ The captain of a World War II submarine looks through the periscope for enemy activity.

"Submariners are a bunch of intelligent misfits that somehow seem to get along, understand each other and work well together."
OVERHEARD SUBMARINE OFFICER

EXECUTIVE DEPARTMENT: The part of a crew that runs a submarine.

Engineers hard at work in the engine room of an Upholder-class Royal Canadian Navy submarine. The Upholder has a diesel-electric engine. They are cheaper to build than nuclear engines, but they are noisier and not as efficient.

▶ Submariners practice in a dive simulator at the Trident Training Facility at Kings Bay, Georgia, USA.

USS KENTUCKY

Crewmembers look out from the sail of USS *Kentucky*. The Ohio-class ballistic missile submarine has been in service since 1991.

DIVE SIMULATOR: A training centre for submarine crew.

SUBMARINE HISTORY

Since the beginning of the 20th century, submarines have played a vital role in warfare. They helped to bring both World Wars to a speedier end. Today, submarines still have an important role to play in both defence and attack.

WWI U-BOAT

Early submarines were very uncomfortable. The working and living spaces were even more cramped than they are today. They were cold and damp, and had no washing facilities.

◀ Crewmen in the engine room of a U-boat in World War I. The whole boat smelled of engine oil.

DETONATION: The action of a bomb exploding.

LUSITANIA SUNK

In World War I, the British passenger liner RMS *Lusitania* left New York for Britain on 1 May 1915. Days later, the Germans declared unrestricted war at sea. U-boat *U-20* torpedoed the *Lusitania*, which sank. Only 764 of the 1,959 people on board survived.

"Shot struck [the] starboard side [of RMS *Lusitania*] close behind the bridge. An extraordinary heavy detonation followed, with a very large cloud of smoke..."
CAPTAIN SCHWIEGER OF U-20

WORLD WAR I

Among the many victims of the sinking of the *Lusitania* were 123 American passengers. Their deaths caused a huge public outcry in the United States. That single hit by a German torpedo was the catalyst for the Americans entering World War I on the side of the Allies.

▲ This painting shows the German U-boat *U-53* sinking the Norwegian cargo vessel *Asheim* in 1917.

WORLD WAR II

At the beginning of World War II, German U-boats attacked Allied supply routes in the Atlantic and Mediterranean. After 1941, the action moved to the Pacific, where U.S. submarines sank Japanese supply vessels.

"No attempt of any kind must be made to rescue members of ships sunk."
ADMIRAL DÖNITZ, ORDERS TO U-BOATS, 1942

U-boats at a German naval dockyard. Early in the war, the U-boats enjoyed great success against Allied merchant shipping. Their crews called the period the 'Happy Time'.

SILENT KILLERS

World War II submarines ran on batteries, because electric engines made almost no noise. The main engine recharged the batteries when the subs were sailing on the surface.

A U.S. submarine prepares to dive in the Pacific Ocean. The defeat of the Japanese Navy left Allied subs free to sink merchant supply ships, leaving the Japanese islands starving.

MERCHANT SHIPS: Unarmed vessels used to carry cargo.

◀ *U-112* surfaces to attack a merchant ship with its guns. Commanders kept torpedoes for attacking warships from underwater.

U-BOAT LIFE

A U-boat crew plays cards to pass the time. Submarine life was uncomfortable, boring and potentially dangerous. Torpedoes, depth charges and bombs were a constant threat.

Many people's idea of life on a submarine comes from the famous German movie *Das Boot* (1981). The film tells the story of the crew of *U-96*. It was a realistic portrayal of life on a U-boat in World War II.

DEPTH CHARGE: A bomb dropped into the sea that blows up underwater.

FALKLANDS

In 1982 Britain went to war when Argentina invaded the Falkland Islands, a tiny British territory in the South Atlantic. Submarines played a key part in the 74-day war that won the islands back for Britain.

> "We, as professionals, said it was just too bad that we lost the Belgrano."
> ARGENTINE REAR ADMIRAL ALLARA

▲ Damaged beneath the waterline, the *General Belgrano* starts to sink on 2 May 1982.

SUNK

Britain's nuclear-powered attack submarine HMS *Conqueror* sank the Argentine cruiser *General Belgrano* with two torpedoes. More than 320 crew died. Fearing more sub attacks, the Argentine Navy stayed in port for the rest of the conflict, which helped Britain gain victory.

▲ HMS *Conqueror* flies the skull and crossbones after sinking the *Belgrano*.

CRUISER: The most powerful type of modern warship.

MODERN WARS

Submarines were used in Operation Enduring Freedom, the 2001 U.S.-led invasion of Afghanistan. From hundreds of kilometres away, subs launched Tomahawk cruise missiles at targets linked with the Taliban and with al-Qaeda terrorists.

▼ The USS *Louisville* passes under the Golden Gate Bridge in San Francisco, California, USA.

NEW SUPPLIES

Nuclear submarines can stay underwater for months, but eventually they have to be re-supplied. They meet up with supply ships to stock up without having to return to harbour.

▲ USS *Greeneville* surfaces at sea to take on food, supplies and personnel.

GALLERY

The biggest submarine fleet in the world belongs to the United States of America. However, many other countries also operate submarines, including Russia, China, Britain and France.

 ## USS *LOUISIANA*

The USS *Louisiana* is one of 18 Ohio-class ballistic missile submarines. The Ohio class forms the main U.S. nuclear deterrent. They have such a long range that they can launch ballistic missiles from any of the world's seas at targets on any continent.

SPECIFICATIONS
Crew: 15 officers, 140 enlisted
Length: 107.7 m (353¼ feet)
Max. speed: 25 knots
Displacement: 17,010 tonnes (18,750 tons)

CLASS: A group of submarines with the same design and armaments.

USS *Toledo* is a Los Angeles-class nuclear-powered fast attack submarine. The class is often used to escort warships and carriers.

SPECIFICATIONS

Crew: 13 officers, 116 enlisted
Length: 109.7 m (360 feet)
Max. speed: 30 knots
Displacement: 6,284 tonnes (6,927 tons)

🇨🇳 **TYPE 093**

SPECIFICATIONS

Crew: Fewer than 100
Length: 110 m (361 feet)
Max. speed: 35 knots
Displacement: 6,000–7,000 tonnes (6,614–7,716 tons)

The Type 093 Shang-class nuclear-powered attack submarine is the latest addition to the Chinese naval fleet. It carries torpedoes and anti-ship missiles.

DISPLACEMENT: A vessel's size, measured by how much water it moves.

GALLERY

🇬🇧 HMS VANGUARD

SPECIFICATIONS
Crew: 143 total
Length: 149.35 m (490 feet)
Max. speed: 25 knots
Displacement: 14,392
   tonnes (15,865 tons)

Britain uses the Vanguard class of nuclear-powered submarines as its nuclear deterrent. At least one of Britain's four Vanguard submarines is at sea at all times, armed with Trident ballistic missiles.

SPECIFICATIONS
Crew: 130
Length: 170 m (557¾ feet)
Max. speed: 29 knots
Displacement: 13,354
   tonnes (14,720 tons)

TRIDENT: A ballistic missile armed with a nuclear warhead.

USS VIRGINIA

The Virginia class is a new generation of submarine. It carries out escort and attack functions and was designed to be cheaper than its predecessors.

SPECIFICATIONS
Crew: 113
Length: 115 m (377 feet)
Max. speed: 25 knots
Displacement: 7,076 tonnes (7,800 tons)

The Borei class is the newest type of nuclear-powered ballistic missile submarine built for the Russian Navy.

BOREI CLASS

PREDECESSOR: An earlier version of something.

GLOSSARY

Allied Relating to the countries that fought Germany in World War II, led by the United States, Britain and the Soviet Union.

al-Qaeda An extremist Islamic terrorist group.

ballistic A long-range, unmanned projectile.

catalyst Something that makes something else happen.

class A group of submarines with the same design and armaments.

claustrophobic Not liking enclosed spaces.

convoy A group of vessels or vehicles all travelling in formation.

cruiser The most powerful type of modern warship.

depth charge A bomb dropped into the sea that explodes underwater.

deterrent A threat that stops someone from acting.

detonation The action of a bomb exploding.

displacement A vessel's size, measured by how much water it moves.

dive simulator A training centre for a submarine crew.

Executive Department The part of a crew that runs a submarine.

merchant ships Unarmed vessels used to carry cargo.

nuclear Powered by energy created by splitting atoms or colliding them together.

Operation Enduring Freedom A global campaign against terrorism.

periscope A tube with mirrors for observing the ocean surface.

predecessor An earlier version of something.

radar A detection system that works by using radio waves.

SEALS U.S. Navy special forces; 'SEALs' stands for 'Sea, Air and Land'.

sonar A tracking system that uses sound to detect activity.

tactical Relating to smaller, short-term operations against the enemy.

Taliban An extremist Islamic group in Afghanistan.

Trident A ballistic missile armed with a nuclear warhead.

U-boat Short for 'Unterseeboot', a German submarine.

warhead The explosive part of a missile.

watch A naval word for a shift, or a period spent at work.

FURTHER READING

BOOKS

Abramson, Andra Serlin. *Submarines Up Close.* Sterling, 2008.

Bodden, Valerie. *Submarines* (Built for Battle). Creative Education, 2012.

Frith, Alex. *Submarines* (Beginners Plus). Usborne Publishing, 2011.

Gilpin, Daniel. *Modern Warships and Submarines* (Machines Close-up). Wayland, 2013.

Langley, Andrew. *Submarines* (Machines on the Move). Franklin Watts, 2011.

Mahaney, Ian F. *Extreme Submarines* (Extreme Machines). PowerKids Press, 2015.

Samuels, Charlie. *World War II* (Machines that Won the War). Wayland, 2014.

WEBSITES

www.ahctv.com/modern-warfare/videos/at-sea-life-on-a-submarine/
Step inside of the Control Room and see what life is like onboard a nuclear military submarine.

http://www.royalnavy.mod.uk/our-organisation/the-fighting-arms/submarine-service
Royal Navy website covering many aspects of British military submarines.

http://science.howstuffworks.com/transport/engines-equipment/submarine.htm
How Stuff Works guide to the design of submarines.

http://military.discovery.com/technology/vehicles/submarines/submarines-intro.html
Military Channel website listing Top 10 submarines of all time.

INDEX